The science in...

...a GUITAR

The science of sound and more...

Anna Claybourne

W

FRANKLIN WATTS

LONDON•SYDNEY

First published in 2008
by Franklin Watts

Copyright © Franklin Watts 2008

Franklin Watts
338 Euston Road
London NW1 3BH

Franklin Watts Australia
Level 17/207 Kent Street
Sydney, NSW 2000

Planning and production by
Discovery Books Limited
Editor: Rebecca Hunter
Designer: Keith Williams
Illustrator: Stefan Chabluk
Photo researcher: Tom Humphrey

Dewey number 534

ISBN 978 0 7496 8241 5

Printed in China

Franklin Watts is a division of Hachette
Children's Books, an Hachette Livre UK
company. www.hachettelivre.co.uk

Photo acknowledgements: istockphoto.com/Dane
Wirtzfeld, front cover top; istockphoto.com/Ernest Fan,
front cover bottom left; istockphoto.com/Arik Chan,
front cover bottom right & p. 19; Corbis/Mimmo
Jodice, p. 4; istockphoto.com, p. 5; istockphoto.com,
p. 6; Corbis/Fernando Bengoechea/Beateworks,
p. 7; Corbis/Gary Houlder, p. 8; istockphoto.com/
Joze Pojbic, p.9; istockphoto.com/Rob Friedman,
p. 11 top; Corbis/Aero Graphics Inc., p. 11 bottom;
istockphoto.com/Jose Gil, p. 13 top; Corbis/
Underwood & Underwood, p. 13 bottom; Corbis/Kelly
Mooney Photography, p. 14; istockphoto.com/Roberto
A. Sanchez, p. 15; istockphoto.com/Jaimie Duplass,
p. 17; Corbis/Neal Preston, p. 18; istockphoto.com,
p. 20; istockphoto.com/Annett Vauteck, p. 21 top;
istockphoto.com/Lisa F. Young, p. 21 bottom; Corbis/
Kevin Dodge, p. 22; Corbis/Owen Franken, p. 23;
Corbis/Sylvain Safra/Hemis, p. 24; istockphoto.com,
p. 25; istockphoto.com/Nathan McClunie, p. 26;
Corbis/Victor Fraile/Reuters, p. 27; Corbis/Marc Bryan-
Brown, p. 28; istockphoto.com/Oleg Prikhodko, p. 29
top; Getty Images/John MacDougall, p. 29 bottom.

Contents

Words that appear in **bold**
are in the glossary on page 30.

What is a guitar?

When did you last hear the strumming sound of a guitar? It was probably today! The guitar features in a lot of the music we hear around us all the time. It's on the radio, TV, records and films. Many people can play the guitar and have one at home. So how does a guitar work? How does it make sound – and music?

Strings on a box

A guitar is basically made of a box with strings fixed to it. The strings are pulled tight, and you play them by plucking them. This means pulling at a string gently, then letting it go.

Instruments similar to guitars have existed for thousands of years. They did not always look exactly like a modern guitar, but they worked in the same way. For example, the ancient Greeks and Romans used an instrument called a cithara that worked like a guitar. In India, people have been playing guitar-like instruments known as sitars for over 5,000 years.

▼ *This painting from ancient Rome, dating from about 2,000 years ago, shows a person playing a cithara.*

Music in our lives

Even if you don't play music yourself, you'll hear it all the time. Pop songs can be heard everywhere. We sing songs at school, and at celebrations such as birthdays. Humans have been singing, dancing and playing instruments for thousands upon thousands of years. Most of us love music – it can cheer you up, pass the time and help people work and have fun together.

Try it yourself

If you have a guitar at home or in your classroom, you can use it to try out some of the things described in this book. If not, you can make a very simple guitar by stretching some large elastic bands over an empty tissue box. You can pluck them like real guitar strings to make sounds.

How sounds work

Music is made of sound – and sound is made by air moving. In this book, you can discover how guitars, and other things, make sounds. You can also find out why some kinds of sounds make music.

Soundhole

Body

Strings

Neck

Soundbox

▲ *This is an **acoustic guitar**, a basic wooden guitar. It has six strings, attached to a curved, hollow wooden body with a long neck. The player plucks the strings with one hand, and presses on them with the other to make different notes.*

Making a sound

The gentle strumming of a guitar; the crash of a drum; hands clapping; a plate smashing or the rumble of thunder... These sounds are all very different, but they all happen in exactly the same way. They are made when something makes the air vibrate, or shake to and fro.

Vibrating strings

If you pluck a single guitar string, then look at it closely, you will see it vibrating. It shakes back and forth very quickly, which makes it look blurred.

As the string vibrates, it pushes at the air around it. Air, like other substances, is made up of tiny parts called **molecules**. As the vibrating string pushes against them, it makes them vibrate too. The vibrations spread out through the air, and when they reach our ears, we hear a sound.

String sounds

Of course, not all strings sound the same. A guitar sounds very different from a violin. They both sound very different from a piano. Even on one guitar, you can make many different sounds.

These different sounds depend on many different things. What the string is made of, how long it is, how tight it is, how thick it is, and how it is played all affect the sound.

▶ *You pluck a string by gently pulling on it and then letting it go. This makes the guitar string vibrate.*

Stringed instruments

Guitars aren't the only instruments that use vibrating strings. Violins and cellos have strings too. You play them by pulling a bow made of fine hairs across them. And did you know that a piano is a stringed instrument, too? When you press the keys, a set of felt hammers hits a set of steel strings. The hammers rebound immediately, allowing the string to continue vibrating. These vibrations are amplified by a **soundboard** so that we can hear them.

▲ *In this photo you can see the strings inside a grand piano.*

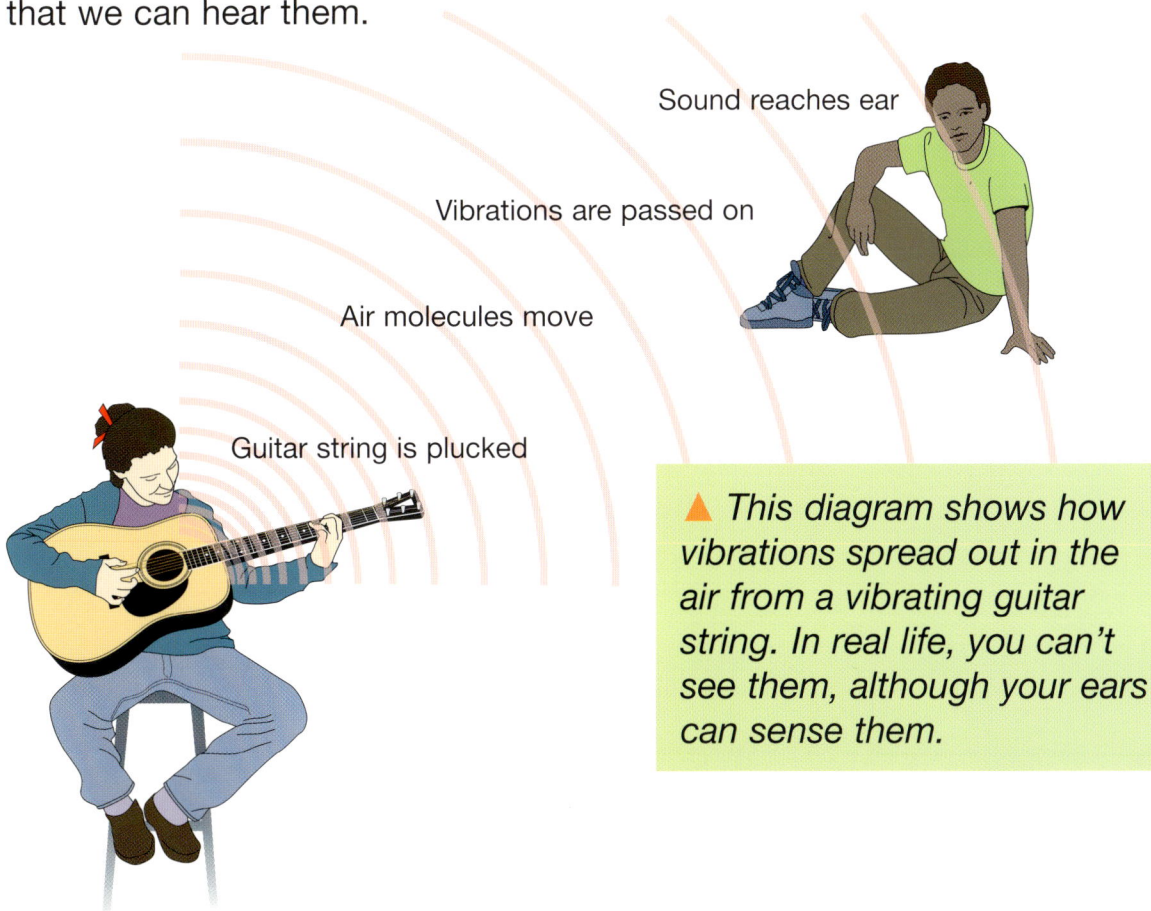

Sound reaches ear

Vibrations are passed on

Air molecules move

Guitar string is plucked

▲ *This diagram shows how vibrations spread out in the air from a vibrating guitar string. In real life, you can't see them, although your ears can sense them.*

Sounds all around

Shhhh! What can you hear right now? If you listen carefully, you're sure to hear something. It could be your hands on the pages of this book, a computer humming, people talking, traffic nearby or just your own breathing. All around us, things are making the air vibrate and making sounds.

Shaking air

All kinds of objects can make noises by making the air vibrate. For example, car engines, washing machines and lawnmowers are noisy because they vibrate as they work. When you talk, air blows through your throat, making parts of it vibrate to make sound.

An object doesn't even have to vibrate itself to make the air vibrate. Try clapping your hands loudly. They don't vibrate, but the clapping pushes some air sideways suddenly. This pushes against the air next to it, setting up a vibration.

▼ *We use clapping to make a loud noise when we applaud a performance.*

Fading away

The air around you is hardly ever completely still. It's constantly buzzing with sound vibrations from here, there and everywhere. However hard you try, if you can hear and are not deaf, it is almost impossible to hear no sound at all. It is always there.

Luckily, though, once a sound has been made, it doesn't stay around for ever. After you pluck a guitar string, the vibrations get weaker and weaker as they spread out through the air. Finally the air stops shaking and returns to normal. If this didn't happen, all the sounds ever made would still be echoing around!

The sound of silence

There is one place that's completely quiet – a **vacuum**. A vacuum is a space with nothing at all in it – no air, water or any substance at all. Sound can only travel if there are molecules that can vibrate. In a vacuum, there are no molecules of any kind. So there is nothing to vibrate, and sound vibrations cannot spread out.

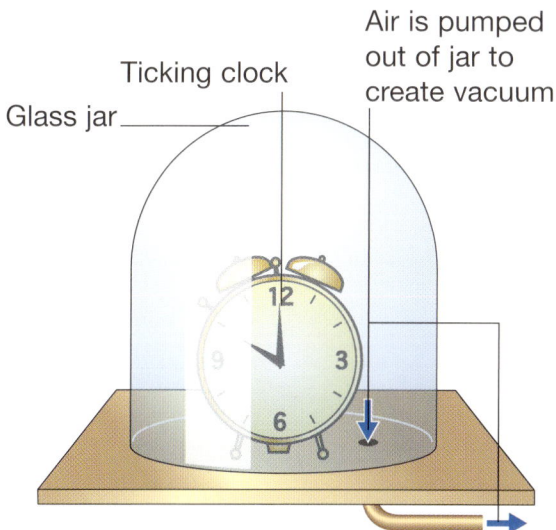

▲ Noisy machines such as chainsaws make such strong sound vibrations that they can damage your ears. This logger is wearing ear defenders to keep the sound out.

Glass jar
Ticking clock
Air is pumped out of jar to create vacuum

◄ In this well-known experiment, you put a ticking clock inside a jar and pump all the air out to make a vacuum. As the air is removed, the sound stops, though you can still see the clock working.

Waves of sound

As sound vibrations spread out, they travel in waves. Think of throwing a pebble into a pond. You see small waves, or ripples, spreading out in circles all around it. Sound works the same way. But instead of spreading out across a flat surface, sound waves spread out through the air in every direction.

How sound waves work

Sound waves spread out just like ripples in water – but they are a different kind of wave. Water waves make the molecules in the water move up and down. But sound waves make the molecules in the air move back and forth. In each wave, some of the molecules are squashed tightly together, and some are spaced out. If you could see a sound wave, it would look like this.

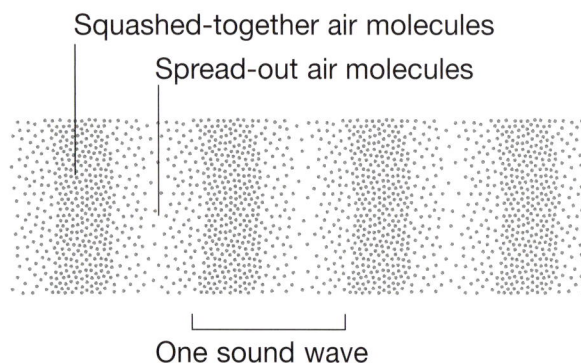

Squashed-together air molecules

Spread-out air molecules

One sound wave

Sound is energy

Sound is a form, or type, of **energy**. Energy comes in many forms, such as movement, light, heat and electricity. All types of energy make something happen or work. Energy can't be made from nothing, and it can't be destroyed. It can only change from one form to another.

So, for example, when you pluck a guitar string, you make it vibrate. This movement energy changes into sound energy, in the form of a sound wave. Where does the sound energy go? As sound waves fade, they change into heat energy. They make the surrounding air very slightly warmer (but not so much that you can feel it).

▲ *This kind of wave is called a **longitudinal wave**. That simply means it moves along the direction it is going in, instead of bobbing up and down like a sea wave.*

▲ The speed of sound means that if you are watching this player from a seat 170 metres away, you will hear the sound of the bat hitting the ball about half a second after it happens.

The speed of sound

Sound waves zoom through the air at about 1,230 km/h. That's fast – much faster than a fast car or train. But you can sometimes see how long sound takes to travel. If you watch someone a long way from you hitting a ball with a bat, you will hear nothing at first. The sound will reach you a second or two later.

▼ Supersonic planes like these can fly faster than the speed of sound. As they fly past, you hear a booming noise as the sound waves all catch up with each other and join together.

How we hear

So when you pluck a guitar string, the vibrations spread out as sound waves. And when those sound waves reach your ears, you hear the sound of a guitar. But how? Your ears aren't just those swirly bits on the sides of your head. Inside is a set of parts that work together to soak up sounds and send them to your brain.

In your ears

As you know, sound is made of tiny air molecules vibrating. Inside your ear is a part called the eardrum. It is made of a thin, tightly stretched skin, a bit like the skin of a drum. As sound waves enter the ear, the moving air molecules actually bump against the eardrum. This makes it vibrate, too.

The eardrum is linked to more parts inside the ear, and they start vibrating as well. Deep inside the ear is a snail-shaped part, the cochlea. It is filled with liquid and lined with tiny hairs. When the liquid vibrates, it makes the hairs move. The hairs are linked to pathways called **nerves**, leading into the brain. They turn the movements into signals that the brain can understand.

▼ *This diagram shows the parts that make up an ear.*

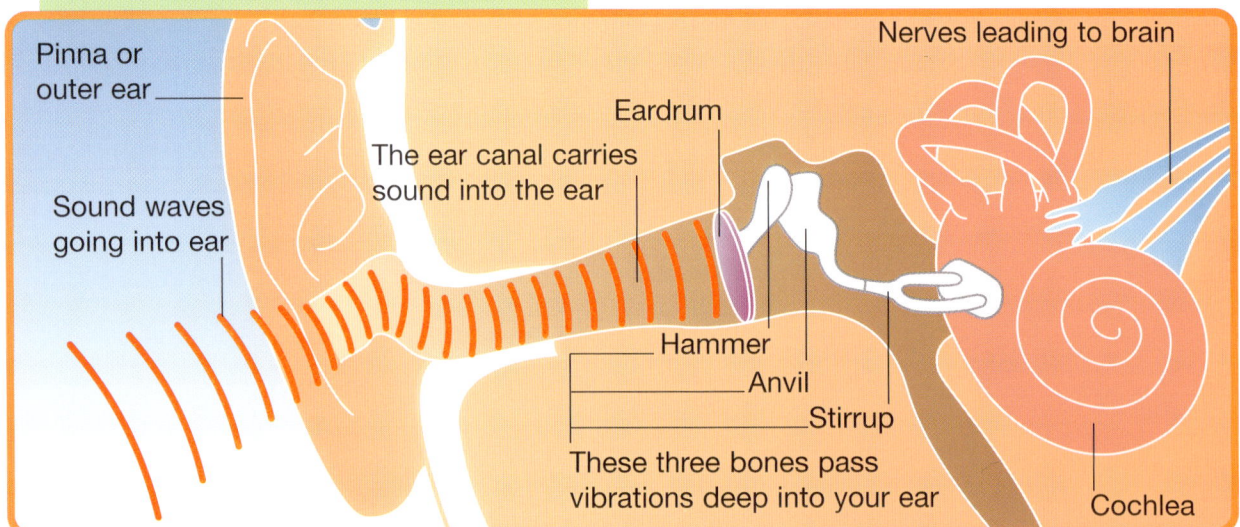

Pinna or outer ear

Sound waves going into ear

The ear canal carries sound into the ear

Eardrum

Nerves leading to brain

Hammer

Anvil

Stirrup

These three bones pass vibrations deep into your ear

Cochlea

▲ *This antelope has extremely large outer ears for catching very faint sounds. Its life depends on hearing predators coming, in time to run away.*

In your brain

Your brain plays a big part in helping you hear. It takes in all the different patterns of sound, and makes sense of them. It can work out whether you're hearing a guitar, a trumpet or a piano. It can take the sound of someone talking, sort it out into words and understand what they mean.

Your brain can even tell the difference between background noise, and what's important. That's why you can chat with a friend in a busy café or playground. Your brain just listens to what they are saying, and tunes out the sound of everyone else.

Sound-catchers

The part of your ear that you can see is called the outer ear or pinna. Its strange shape also helps you to hear. The pinna's swirling, curling bowl shape catches sound waves, and bounces them into your ear, towards the eardrum.

When ears don't work

Some people's ears don't work at all, and others lose their hearing as they get older. But if you are deaf (unable to hear), you may still be able to sense the sound of a guitar. You can often feel the vibrations from a musical instrument through your head, feet or other body parts.

After the great composer Ludwig van Beethoven (right) went deaf, he would hold a stick between his teeth and press it against his piano. The sound vibrations passed up the stick and into his head.

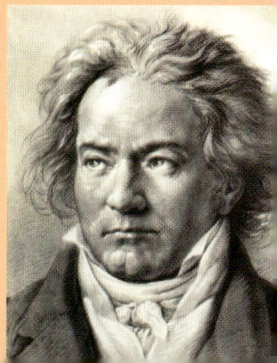

Sound in a box

You already know why guitars have strings. But what about the big, wooden box that the strings are attached to? What's that for? It's called the soundbox, and it makes the sound of a guitar richer, deeper and louder.

Quiet strings

On its own, a vibrating string does not make a very loud noise. If you have an elastic band, try stretching it out in your hands and plucking it. It's pretty quiet! But if you stretch the elastic band over a hollow box, such as a tissue box, and then pluck it, it sounds louder.

A guitar works this way too. The ends of the strings are fixed to the soundbox, which has a round hole in it. When you pluck a string, it passes its vibrations on into the wood of the soundbox. The soundbox starts to vibrate in the same way, or **resonate**. So does the air inside it. This makes a much louder, fuller sound than the string would by itself.

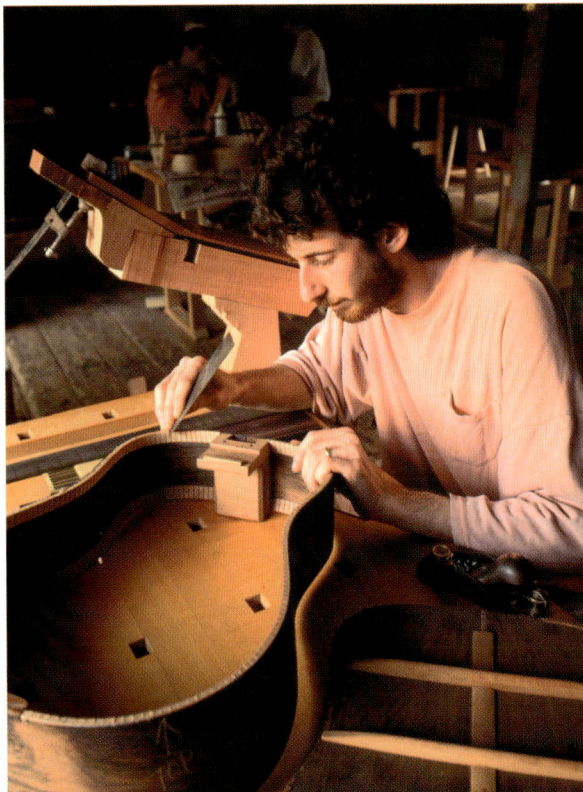

Letting it out

The round hole in a guitar's soundbox is called the **soundhole**. It lets the vibrations from the soundbox spread out into the air.

◄ Guitars have to be built carefully to make sure they are strong enough to support the strings, but light and flexible enough to resonate well.

▲ *A double bass has a soundbox similar to a guitar's, but with two S-shaped soundholes.*

Spot the soundbox

Most musical instruments have a soundbox, or a part that works like one. For example, violins and cellos have wooden bodies, like guitars. Wind instruments have a long, hollow tube with air inside. A drum has a skin that vibrates, with a hollow box-shaped part attached to it.

Hollow hands

You can make your own soundbox with your hands to see what a difference it makes. First, try singing a tune normally. Then cup your hands around your mouth, leaving a small gap. Try singing the same thing again. It sounds fuller and louder because of the air vibrating inside the 'soundbox' you have made.

How loud?

Shhhh! Some sounds are so quiet, you can hardly hear them at all. On the other hand, a thunderclap, a passing plane or even LOUD SHOUTING can make you cover your ears! So what makes sounds loud or quiet?

Turn up the volume!

The volume of a sound means how powerful it is. The higher the volume, the louder a sound seems to our ears.

Volume depends on the strength of the vibrations a sound makes. If the air is vibrating very strongly, the molecules move back and forth faster, and hit your eardrums harder.

▼ *This diagram shows 1) a string vibrating a little; 2) the same string vibrating more widely.*

Your ears sense this as a louder noise. As louder noises carry more energy, they also spread out further into the air, so you can hear them from further away.

On the guitar

If you can, try making sounds of different volumes on a guitar. If you pluck a string gently, it only vibrates a little. It makes the air vibrate gently, so gentle vibrations hit your ears. If you pluck the string hard, it moves further and faster as it vibrates, setting up bigger vibrations in the air.

1 Gentle vibrations: Low sound volume

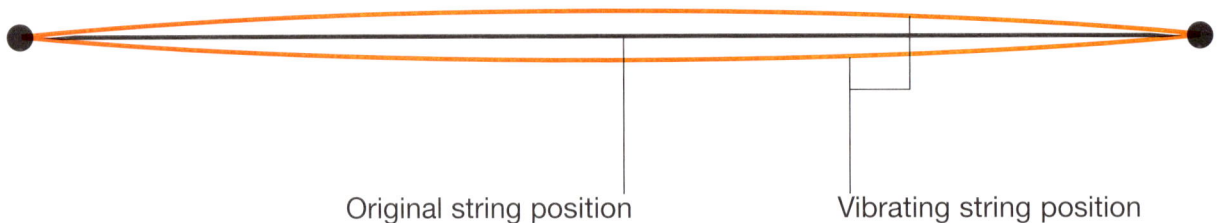

Original string position   Vibrating string position

2 Stronger vibrations: High sound volume

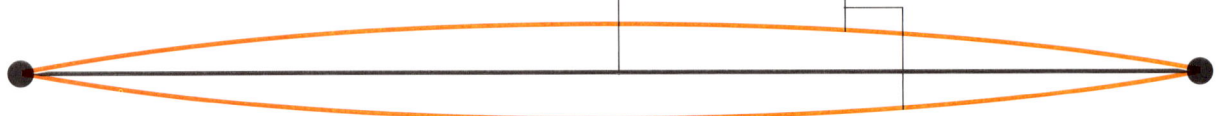

Decibels

Volume is measured in units called decibels (dB for short). The volume of the quietest sound you can hear, such as very faint breathing, is 10 decibels. There is no upper end to the decibel scale. But the loudest sounds on record measure around 180 to 200dB. They include big volcanic eruptions, and the singing of the blue whale. Scientists have also made sounds this loud on purpose, in special sound labs.

Protect your ears!

Very loud sounds can damage your ears and even burst your eardrums. Avoid listening to very loud music through earphones, as it can damage your hearing over time.

▼ *Listening to music on an MP3 player is great fun, but be careful not to listen to it too loud as it can damage your eardrums.*

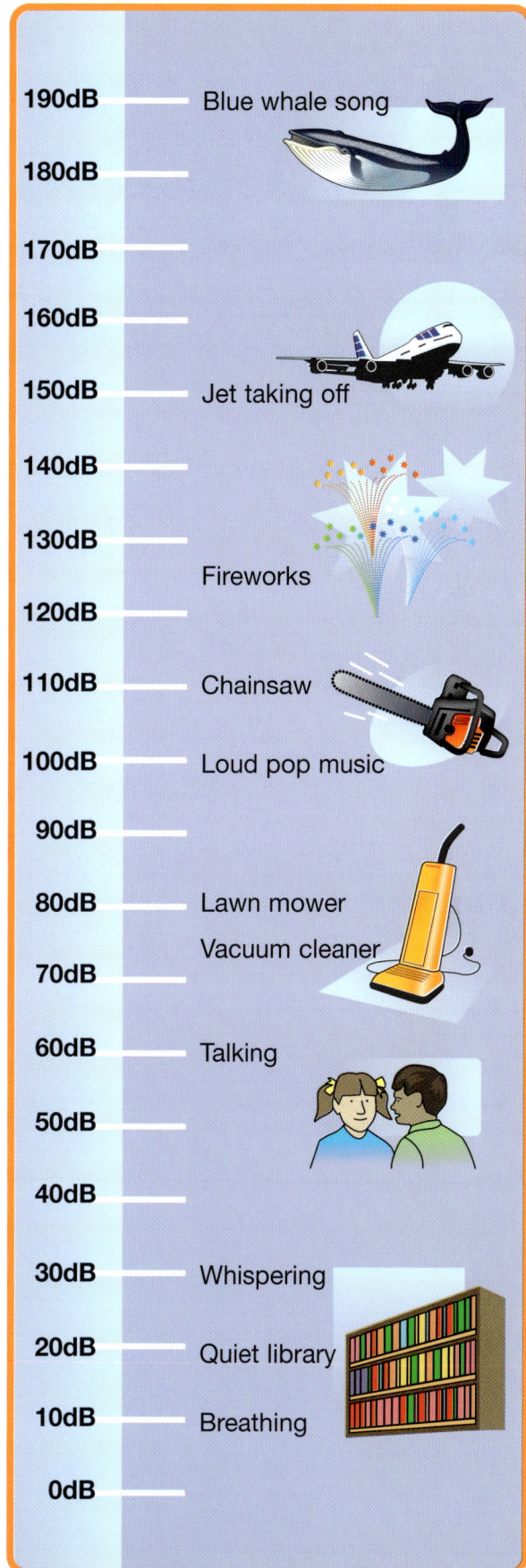

dB	
190dB	Blue whale song
180dB	
170dB	
160dB	
150dB	Jet taking off
140dB	
130dB	Fireworks
120dB	
110dB	Chainsaw
100dB	Loud pop music
90dB	
80dB	Lawn mower
70dB	Vacuum cleaner
60dB	Talking
50dB	
40dB	
30dB	Whispering
20dB	Quiet library
10dB	Breathing
0dB	

Electric guitars

If you look at an electric guitar, you'll see that its body is solid, not hollow. It has no soundbox at all. And yet an electric guitar can be very loud indeed! Electric guitars work in a different way to an acoustic guitar. They use energy from electricity to make them sound loud.

How it works

Where an acoustic guitar has a soundhole, an electric guitar has **pickups**. These are little pads that sense the vibrations from the strings. They turn the vibrations into patterns of electrical signals.

The signals travel along a wire to an **amp** – short for **amplifier**. The amp uses an electricity supply to make the signals stronger, or **amplify** them. It then sends the signals to an electric speaker.

Out of the speaker

Some amps have a speaker built into them. Others connect to a separate speaker. Either way, the speaker's job is to turn the signals back into sounds. It uses the electricity to make a cone inside vibrate back and forth. As in a musical instrument, this vibrating makes the air vibrate, creating a sound.

▼ *A rock band playing electric guitars. The sound is coming out of the speakers behind them.*

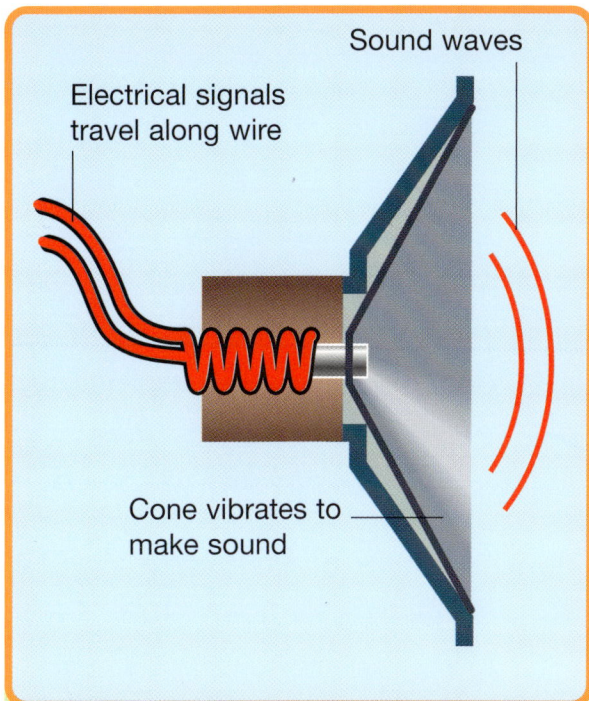

Electrical signals travel along wire

Sound waves

Cone vibrates to make sound

▲ *A speaker turns electrical signals into sound waves.*

Amplifying without electricity

Before electric amps and speakers, people amplified sounds using a cone-shaped loudspeaker. If you talk or play music into the narrow end of a cone, the cone resonates and makes the sound louder. Cone-shaped speakers were used for public speaking and on early record players.

Amplify anything

There are many other electric instruments too, such as **synthesizers** and electric violins. And most instruments can have pickups attached to them, so that their sound can be amplified and played through a speaker. A **microphone** works like a pickup, too. We often use microphones to amplify someone speaking or singing.

▶ *This very old record player does not use electricity at all. A wind-up handle would have turned the turntable, and a metal horn amplified the sound of the record.*

Different notes

When you hear someone playing a guitar, they play lots of notes by moving their fingers around. And if you sing a tune, you sing different notes in order. To make different notes, you have to make sound vibrations faster or slower.

Notes on strings

On a guitar, there are six strings. Each one plays a different note when you pluck it. The notes are all different because the strings are fixed to the guitar differently. Some are stretched more tightly than others. The more tightly a string is stretched, the faster it vibrates. The faster it vibrates, the higher the note it plays. The number of sound waves per second zooming through the air is called the **frequency**. The **pitch** is how high or low the note is.

There's another way to make different notes on a guitar, too. If you press your finger down on a string, somewhere along the neck, you will make the string shorter. When you pluck it, it will have a higher pitch than before. The shorter a string is, the higher the note it plays.

▼ *It is possible to either play single notes or several different notes at the same time, by using several fingers at once to press the strings on the neck.*

Some other instruments make different notes by making a tube longer or shorter.

Notes have names

We give notes names to tell them apart. They are named after the first seven letters of the alphabet – A, B, C, D, E, F and G.

Voice pitch

When we talk or sing, we change the pitch of our voices all the time. This helps us to sing tunes, and also to add meaning to our words. Try saying the word 'No' in a bored way, a shocked way and an angry way. You use changes in pitch – how high or low you speak – to make them sound different.

▲ *A trombone has a tube that moves in and out to change its length. The longer it is, the lower the note.*

Bottle organ

You can make a simple instrument with several different notes, using glass bottles or jars. It works best if you can collect several bottles that are all the same. Fill them with different amounts of water, and they will play different notes when you tap them with a spoon.

◀ *When you learn to sing, you learn to hit the right note with your voice. You do this using your vocal cords – two stringy body parts in your throat. To lower your voice you make them thicker, and to make your voice higher, you make them thinner.*

Sounds like...

Even with your eyes closed, you can recognise thousands of different sounds. You can easily tell a guitar from a trumpet, or a slamming door from a flushing toilet. So what is it that makes musical instruments – and other sounds – so different from each other?

Timbre

When you play a note on a musical instrument, you do not actually play just that note. Different parts of the instrument vibrate in different ways, making several quieter notes, called **harmonics**.

For example, if you pluck the top string on a guitar, you hear the main vibration as the note E. But you will also hear harmonics, and other sounds, such as the echoing of the note inside the soundbox. These give the guitar its own special sound, or **timbre**.

Your voice has its own timbre too. Each person has a slightly different voice, because of the shape of their throat and vocal cords. This helps us to recognise people, even on the phone.

Patterns in the air

Everyday sounds, such as a car engine starting, also have their own special sound patterns. Some people can even tell apart different makes of cars, and different types of birds singing.

But amazingly, every sound in the world is made up of nothing more than patterns of vibrations in the air. We can tell what they are simply from our ears sensing the way the sound waves speed up and down.

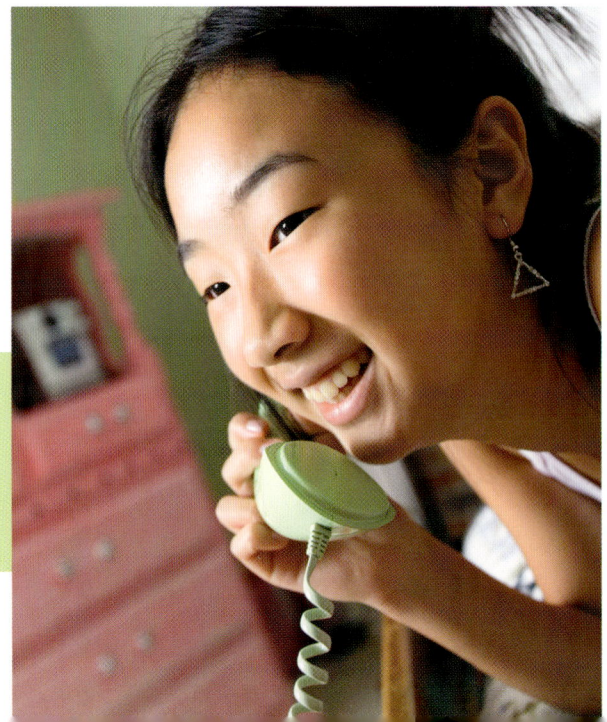

▶ *Even though telephones distort (change) our voices, it's often easy to tell who's calling as soon as they start talking.*

▲ *Some musical instruments are treasured because they have an extra-beautiful sound. This is a 'Stradivarius' violin, made by a man named Antonio Stradivari in the early 1700s. These violins are often worth a lot of money.*

Seeing sounds

A sound can be shown as a kind of diagram, called a **waveform**. A waveform looks like a drawing of a wave. It is a way of showing the patterns of vibrations in a sound wave. Any sound can be shown as a waveform. Here's one example:

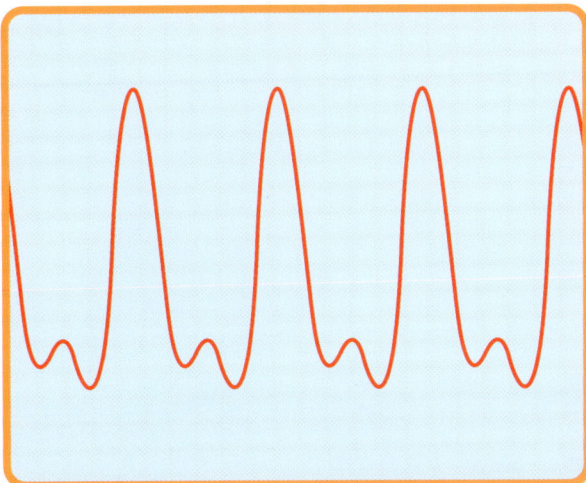

Pure note

Can you imagine what the purest sound of all sounds like? It is just a single, steady vibration, with no other sounds mixed in. The noise it makes sounds a bit like a flute.

◄ *This waveform represents the sound of a trombone note.*

Making music

We listen to our favourite music to make us happy. And of course, music is made up of sounds. It's hard to say exactly what music is, and what makes it different from other sounds. However, most music includes a tune, a rhythm, or beat, and a structure, or shape.

Name that tune

A tune is a set of notes, arranged into an order or sequence. In most tunes, the notes make a pattern of some kind. The same section may repeat over and over, or the notes may run up and down like steps. Try singing or playing some tunes you know, and see if you can spot the patterns in them.

In some kinds of music, such as pop songs, there are words that go with the tune, too. Songs are one of the oldest ways of passing information from generation to generation.

Feel the beat

The rhythm is a steady, repeated beat, like a drum being hit over and over again. The beating of your heart and the sound of your footsteps when you walk make a steady rhythm too. (In fact, these things may explain why humans like rhythm so much!) Most music fits to a regular beat. In pop songs and lots of other music, the rhythm is played on the drums and also on the guitar.

Musical shapes

A song or other piece of music also has an overall shape, or structure. For example, a pop song might start with one tune for the verse, then have a different tune for the chorus. The

▶ Drummers playing at a street carnival in Salvador, Brazil.

Notes   Bars   Stave

Hap-py   birth-day to   you.   Hap-py   birth-day   to

- The pitch of the note is shown by how high or low it is on the stave
- The bars divide the music into sections of time. Each section contains three beats of the rhythm.

verse and chorus could then repeat again and again through the song.

Even a very simple song such as 'Happy Birthday' has its own tune, rhythm and a clear structure. Above you can see part of 'Happy Birthday' written down. The words are written in normal writing. The music is shown using dots arranged on a set of five lines, called a stave.

Types of music

There are thousands of different styles and types of music. They include classical music, pop music, folk music and jazz. On page 31 you can find a link to a website where you can hear some different styles of music played on several types of guitar.

▼ *The banjo is related to the guitar, but makes a more jangly, rattling sound. It is often used to play folk music.*

Sounding sweet

Ugh! What's that terrible noise? Played properly, most music sounds sweet and pleasing. But if you hear someone playing the wrong notes on a guitar, or singing out of tune, it sounds awful! So why are some notes wrong, and some right?

Musical scales

Most music sticks to a particular **key** – a special set of notes that sound good together. For example, the scale of C major is the key you play in if you play only the white notes on a piano. Other keys include some of the black notes.

Some keys have a happy sound, and others sound sad. This means you can choose a scale to suit the music you are making.

When you're playing in a key, you usually stick to the notes of that key. Playing a different note can sound all wrong.

The scale of C Major

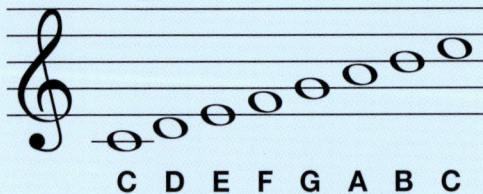

C D E F G A B C

C D E F G A B C

▲ A key has seven main notes in it. The eighth or top note in the scale – C in this case – is the same as the first note, but higher.

▲ On a guitar you can play a **chord** by strumming all the strings together.

▲ This orchestra (see page 28) has around 80 members who must all play together, in time and in tune.

In harmony

In most music, you don't just hear one note at a time. You hear lots of notes together. For example, a guitarist often strums the strings, playing them all at once. This makes a chord, a group of notes played together.

When two or more notes or tunes are played together, it's called **harmony**. Some notes sound good played together – others sound wrong, or **discordant**. Composers, who write music, and people who play it, have to know which is which so that their music sounds right.

Sounding wrong on purpose

In the 20th century, some composers began to experiment with 'wrong', or discordant, notes and harmonies. They put them into their music on purpose, to make it sound strange.

The Austrian-American composer Arnold Schoenberg and the German composer Karlheinz Stockhausen were two examples. They both used a lot of discord in their music.

4'33"

In 1952, the composer John Cage wrote a piece of music called 4'33". Any instrument or instruments can play it, including the guitar. The music tells the player to do nothing at all for 4 minutes and 33 seconds. As the musician sits there silently, the audience must listen to the other sounds going on around them.

Playing together

You can make great music just playing a single guitar by itself. But guitars, like other instruments, are often played as part of a group. It could be a pop or rock band, a folk group or a full-sized orchestra.

The pop band line-up

One reason guitars are so well-known and widespread is that most pop bands have a guitar. A typical pop band is made up of a singer, a guitarist, a drummer and a bass guitarist. A bass guitar has only four strings and plays very low, deep notes in the background, while the lead guitar plays tunes and chords.

Some pop singers, though, perform on their own, playing a guitar and singing along to it.

In the orchestra

An orchestra is a very large group of musicians who play together. Instead of short songs, they usually play long pieces of classical music, called symphonies. An orchestra can have over 80 members, including violin and cello players, clarinet and flute players, trumpeters, trombonists and drummers. To help them all play together, they have a **conductor** to lead them. He or she waves a stick called a **baton** to show the rhythm of the music.

◄ *Guitars do not play in most orchestras. But some composers have written pieces called* **concertos** *for a solo guitarist playing with an orchestra, and pop bands sometimes play with orchestras too.*

In concert

Bands and orchestras often put on public performances or concerts. People can come and hear the music live, instead of on a CD. The players have to watch and listen to each other carefully, to make sure they all play their parts at the right moments.

Concert halls are specially shaped to make the sounds bounce right to the back so that everyone can hear. At a pop concert, the band usually uses electric amplifiers and speakers. A sound engineer controls the sounds coming out of the speakers to make sure the music sounds just right.

▲ This is the bass guitarist in a pop band. His guitar has an extra-long neck and four thick strings, rather than six.

▼ A sound engineer uses all these buttons and dials to mix the sounds coming out of the speakers, so that a good balance of all the different instruments comes out. This sound engineer is working in a recording studio, where bands record their songs to make records.

That could be you!

Would you like to be up on the stage playing music at a live concert or pop gig? If you don't play an instrument already, why not think about learning one? You could ask your school or parents about choosing an instrument and starting lessons.

Glossary

acoustic guitar a basic wooden guitar

amp short for 'amplifier'

amplifier a device that makes electrical sound signals more powerful

amplify to make louder

baton a small stick used by a conductor to beat the rhythm of a piece of music

chord a set of notes played at the same time

concerto a piece of music for a solo instrument accompanied by an orchestra

conductor someone who leads and directs the musicians in an orchestra to help them play

discordant used to describe musical notes that sound wrong together

energy something that makes things happen or work. Electricity, light and sound are all forms of energy.

frequency in a sound, the number of sound waves per second

harmonics quieter notes that an instrument makes alongside its main note

harmony two or more notes or tunes being played together

key a set of notes that go well together, used for playing a tune or piece of music

longitudinal wave a wave, like a sound wave, that vibrates in the same direction as it travels

microphone a device that collects sounds such as a singer's voice in order to amplify them

molecules tiny particles that substances are made up of

nerves pathways connecting the brain to the rest of the body

pickups devices that sense sound vibrations and turn them into electrical signals

pitch how high or low a note or sound is

resonate to vibrate at the same speed as another object

rhythm the beat of a piece of music

soundboard a thin sheet of wood positioned under the strings in an instrument, such as a piano, to increase the sound produced

soundhole the round hole in a guitar

structure the shape of something such as a piece of music

synthesizer an instrument that creates sounds electronically

timbre the individual sound of an instrument or voice

vacuum a completely empty space

waveform a diagram showing a sound in the form of a picture of a wave

Further information

Websites

Instruments in Depth: the Guitar

http://www.bsmny.org/features/
iidguitar/index.php

*An illustrated introduction to the guitar,
including sound samples of different
types of guitars and guitar music.*

Creating Music

http://www.creatingmusic.com/

*A children's online creative music
environment with music games,
puzzles and recordings.*

John Cage's 4'33"

http://interglacial.com/~sburke/stuff/
cage_433.html

*Listen to John Cage's famous short
piece of music 4'33"*

Note to parents and teachers: *Every effort
has been made by the publishers to ensure
that these websites are suitable for children,
that they are of the highest educational value,
and that they contain no inappropriate or
offensive material. However, because of the
nature of the Internet, it is impossible to
guarantee that the contents of these sites
will not be altered. We strongly advise that
Internet access is supervised by a
responsible adult.*

Index